Swim Like a Fish

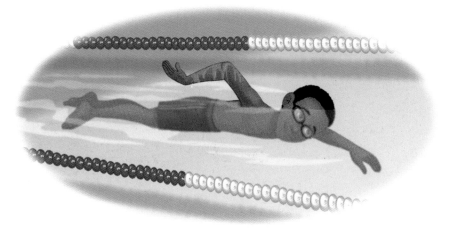

Written by Kerrie Shanahan
Illustrated by Omar Aranda

Flying Start
to Literacy®

Contents

Chapter 1

A special friendship

For as long as Jake could remember, he had been best friends with his next-door neighbour, Mason. Mason was a year older than Jake and they had grown up together, almost like brothers. They were always together: kicking the soccer ball, playing hide-and-seek in Mason's yard, playing around in Jake's pool or just hanging out.

One day Mason came next door and asked Jake if he wanted to join his hiking club.

"I think you'll really like it, Jake."

"What do you do there?" Jake looked up with interest.

"Well, we meet once a week," Mason explained excitedly. "We learn all about the outdoors and we play games and run in relay races. We go camping and hiking and do all sorts of cool stuff. My dad is one of the leaders and the other kids are really friendly."

The best memories Jake had of his friendship with Mason were the times they went camping together with Mason's dad. Jake loved these camping trips more than anything. He loved getting out in nature and setting up camp.

Mason's dad knew all about the outdoors and he taught the boys how to put up the tent, find fresh water and make a camp fire.

Jake knew he would love the hiking club, but he tried not to get too excited just yet.

"That sounds great, but I'll have to check with my dad."

When Jake asked his dad if he could join Mason's hiking club, his dad immediately and firmly said no.

"You haven't got time, Jake. You have swimming training to think of now. You have to be committed."

"But . . . but, I . . . " Jake began to argue with his father's decision, but his voice trailed off. He knew it was pointless.

And that was the end of that.

Chapter 2

Jake "the Fish"

Jake was a swimmer. He had always loved to swim. He began swimming lessons as a baby and Jake's mum said that he was the best swimmer in the class. One of Jake's favourite photographs is a blurry snapshot of his mum in the pool with him. He was wearing bright red swim shorts and a wide, proud smile.

As Jake got older, he kept on swimming and began "real" swimming lessons in the big pool with children much older than he was. Jake still clearly remembers his teacher, Frances. She always made Jake feel like he could do anything and everything, and Jake loved to make her proud. In fact, it was Frances who gave Jake his nickname. She would say, "Here comes the Fish" and "There goes the Fish". And so Jake became known as "the Fish" – and the name stuck!

Before long, Jake was picked to be in the swimming
team at his local swim club. He was seven years old and
he was the youngest boy to ever make the team. Jake
loved competing in races and he loved cheering on his
teammates. Most of all, he loved to win and make his
parents and coaches proud of him.

When Jake turned eleven, his swimming became a lot
more serious. Jake was fast and his technique was good.
Everyone said he was a natural and had the potential to
be a champion.

So Jake's dad took charge and hired a personal coach for Jake. Jake's new coach, Max, had the knowledge and experience to turn Jake into a champion. He was an Olympian.

When Jake first met Max, he immediately recognised him. He remembered seeing him standing on the podium at an Olympic ceremony, being presented with a gold medal.

Wow, thought Jake as he shook Max's hand. This is serious now!

Jake trained diligently, arriving at the pool early in the morning and swimming laps when everyone else was still tucked up in bed. Max worked on carefully perfecting Jake's technique.

"It's the tiny things that make a massive difference." This was Max's motto and each time he said it, Jake would nod in agreement.

And so Jake got even better. He loved the feeling of diving into the water and cutting through it with his strong arms. He loved knowing that with each stroke he pulled his body faster and faster towards the finish line, and towards his goal of becoming a champion.

Jake was always busy with swimming commitments – training or doing his fitness and exercise routine, or at swimming competitions. And, the faster Jake went in the pool, the busier he became and the less time he had to spend with his friend Mason.

Chapter 3

A goal is set

Jake hid his disappointment about not joining Mason's hiking club. Maybe Dad was right. He had to be committed to swimming if he was going to be a great swimmer. Jake started training every day, and spent longer and longer in the pool.

And it paid off. He was getting faster and faster, and he kept smashing his personal best times.

"If you keep working hard, Jake," said Max enthusiastically, "you could swim fast enough to make the state team."

"The state team!" Jake's eyes widened. "That'd be pretty cool!"

Now Jake had a goal! He was determined to work even harder so he could qualify for the state team. His coach, his dad, his mum, Mason and even his little sister Amy all hoped that Jake would make it! Jake loved the attention and he especially loved it that his mum and dad were so proud of him.

But, sometimes he felt worried and this frustrated him. Why was he worried when he should be so happy?

One day, the local newspaper wrote an article about Jake.

The Daily Times

Jake "the Fish" – Our Next Swimming Champion?

After that, everyone knew about Jake's goal. Jake's friends knew, his teacher knew, even Jake's principal knew.

"I hope you make the state team," she encouraged him. "And I can't wait to see you at the Olympic Games."

When Jake went shopping with his mum and dad, strangers would recognise him and say, "You're Jake the Fish, aren't you? Good luck with making the team!"

Jake automatically smiled, but then that worried feeling slowly settled on him like a cold, wet cloud. And this time Jake recognised what the feeling was. It was pressure! He tried to shake it off, but he couldn't.

Everyone thought Jake was confident and never got nervous, but Jake knew that wasn't entirely true. If he really examined his feelings, he would have to admit that he was feeling nervous. He felt pressure to swim fast. He felt pressure to win. And he felt pressure not to let everyone down. He didn't want to disappoint his mum, or his dad, or his coach Max. And he didn't want to disappoint his school or principal. He didn't want to disappoint anyone.

Jake took a deep, shaky breath. "I'll just have to work harder," he told himself determinedly. "Then I won't let anyone down."

Chapter 4

An exciting invitation

A few weeks before the state trials, Mason raced next door with some exciting news that he just had to share with Jake.

"Jake!" he called. "Guess what I'm doing for my birthday? Dad's going to take you, me, Tim and Ben camping at Misty Mountain. We'll go hiking and canoeing and it'll be so much fun. I just can't wait."

"Wow!" Jake was excited too. "That'll be great!"

At dinner that night, Jake eagerly told his family all about Mason's birthday plans.

"Hold it there, Jake," interrupted his dad. "There's no way you can go. The trip is one week before your swimming competition and you know how important it is."

"That doesn't matter. I can still swim in the competition." Jake looked from his dad to his mum, pleading with his eyes. "Please, can I go?"

"No. You'll have training. Plus, you won't sleep that well in a tent. And you might catch a cold or something!"

"But that's not fair!" Jake was suddenly furious. "It's Mason's birthday and I'm his best friend!"

Jake jumped out of his chair and ran to his room.

That night, just before bedtime, Jake's dad came into his bedroom. "Jake? I know you're upset, but I need to talk to you."

Jake looked away. He was still angry.

"I'm sorry I said no to Mason's camping trip." His dad sighed as he sat on the edge of the bed. "Your mum and I discussed it further and we've changed our minds. We've decided that you can go on Mason's camping trip, after all."

Jake's mood changed in a heartbeat. "Really? You're serious?" His eyes were wide with excitement.

"Yes," smiled Jake's dad. "You've been training so hard, you deserve some fun. But promise me you'll be careful. No injuries!"

"Thanks, Dad!" Jake gave his dad a big hug.

That night as Jake drifted off to sleep, he felt content and happy as he thought about the upcoming camping trip with Mason. But, without warning, that familiar nervous feeling came over him.

What if I do get injured? he thought. What if I ruin my chances of getting into the state team? What would Dad, and Mum, and Max think then?

Jake struggled to push these thoughts from his mind as he tossed and turned through the night.

Chapter 5

A decision for Jake

The boys had an amazing time at Misty Mountain. They hiked up the mountain and saw animals living in the forest. They canoed on the lake and caught some fish. At night, they cooked marshmallows on the campfire. But, like all fun times, it felt like it was over in a flash and before the boys knew it, they were packing up camp.

"This has been the best birthday ever," said Mason sincerely as he and Jake took down their tent. "Thanks for coming Jake. It wouldn't have been the same without you."

"I wouldn't have missed it for anything!" replied Jake. "Now! I'll race you to that big tree over there!"

The boys raced to the tree, with big grins on their faces. Jake flew across the ground and, just as he reached for the tree, he slipped on a rock and lost balance. Thud!

"Ahh!" groaned Jake.

"Jake!" Mason turned in shock.
"Are you all right?"

Tim, Ben and Mason's dad all rushed over.

"I'm fine!" Jake stood up quickly.

The boys sighed with relief.

"Come on, Fish!" Mason's dad put an arm around his shoulders. "It's time to get you home safely. You have a big swimming competition coming up!"

"I sure do!" Jake forced his mouth into a smile.

What Jake hadn't told Mason and the others, however, was that he wasn't fine. He wasn't fine at all. He had hurt himself when he slipped on that rock. He had landed on his wrist and bent it backwards, jarring it badly. And the pain was reminding him how silly he had been.

On the trip home, Jake pursed his lips together to stop himself from crying.

I have to swim in two days' time, Jake's mind raced. I have to swim. I can't let everyone down.

But he could barely move his wrist without it hurting!

If Dad finds out, he'll be so disappointed with me, thought Jake. And he'll never let me go camping again!

It was then that Jake knew exactly what he had to do.

Chapter 6

The state trials

On the day of the state trials, Jake woke up early with a start. His stomach did an involuntary flip as he realised what day it was and what was ahead of him. Then Jake remembered his injury and immediately looked at his wrist. The swelling had gone down.

He cautiously moved his injured wrist back and forth. It hurt a little but, surprisingly, it wasn't too bad. Good, Jake thought with relief. I will be able to swim. And no one will ever know about my injury.

Jake had been hiding his sore wrist from everyone since the camping trip. For two days now, he had tried not to move it. When he was alone in his bedroom, he raised his wrist high on a pillow on his desk and put an ice pack on it. All the rest and ice had definitely helped.

And now, it looked like he had got away with it – no one had noticed that he had hurt his wrist.

You can do it, Fish! Jake talked positively in his head.

Jake did well in the first race, but not as well as everyone had expected or hoped.

"Is everything okay, Jake?" Max had quizzed Jake.

"Yeah." Jake avoided his coach's earnest look. "I'm just warming up."

Jake knew that his sore wrist was probably stopping him from swimming his fastest.

"It's the tiny things that make a massive difference."
Max's words kept going around and around in Jake's mind.

Jake swam fast in the next few races, but not fast enough.
He didn't swim his fastest times and he didn't make the
state team.

Although Jake had desperately wanted to make the state
team, he was actually not that disappointed. In fact,
strangely, he almost felt relieved. Maybe now Dad will let
me join Mason's hiking club, he thought.

"Bad luck, Fish," said his coach. "Maybe next year."

"Don't worry," said Jake's mum. "You've worked very
hard and we're all proud of you."

Jake smiled broadly and was feeling like everything was
actually working out for the best. And then Jake realised
that his dad had not spoken to him.

Dad must be really disappointed, thought Jake glumly,
as they walked to the car.

And now Jake felt really guilty.

That night, Jake's dad came to say good night to Jake.

"I know about your wrist," said Jake's dad.

Jake took a short, sharp breath. His mouth went dry and he couldn't speak. He stared up at his dad with big, round eyes.

"I saw you holding it after your final swim," continued his dad. "I'm guessing that you hurt it on the camping trip?"

"Yes," said Jake in a small voice. He swallowed hard and thought he was about to cry.

"It was brave of you to swim with an injury," said Jake's dad. "But you should have told us! You could have made it much worse and then you would have been out of swimming for a long time."

"I couldn't tell you!" Jake rubbed his injured wrist.
"I didn't want to let you down. I know how much you, and Mum, and Max wanted me to make the state team. Plus, I was worried you wouldn't let me go camping again."

"But you wanted to make the state team too, didn't you Jake?" Jake's dad was puzzled.

"Of course I did," Jake said quickly. "It's just that I want to do other normal stuff too, like Mason does."

"Really?" Jake's dad looked surprised. "Well, I guess we will have to think about that. Good night, Fish."

"Good night, Dad."

* * * * *

A week later, Jake was bursting with excitement.

"Thanks for letting me join Mason's hiking club, Dad."
Jake kept looking at his watch. He couldn't wait to
get there.

"As Max said, one night off training won't hurt you and
as your mum says, you need to have fun, too." Jake's dad
smiled at his son.

"I know, Dad, and when I'm at training I'll work even
harder," promised Jake.

"You know, I'm proud of you, Fish." Jake's dad was suddenly serious. "In *and* out of the pool!"

Jake looked at his shoes and smiled.

Beep! Beep! The sound of a car horn broke the silence.

"That's Mason's dad!" Jake raced down the stairs.

"Have fun, Fish!"

"Thanks, Dad. I will!"

A note from the author

When I was growing up, my best friend was amazing at tennis. By the age of 13, she was the best female player in our town. She had a coach, trained really hard and played in tournaments all over the country. She had heaps of potential and everyone thought that she might become a professional tennis player.

There were many times when my friend had to miss out on doing lots of "normal" things with her friends. I know this was hard on her!

Today, I have a friend whose son is an excellent swimmer. She drives him to early morning training four times a week and he swims in lots of competitions.

By mixing what I knew about these friends, I came up with the idea for this story and the character of Jake was born. I wonder if you know anyone like Jake?